AF334982

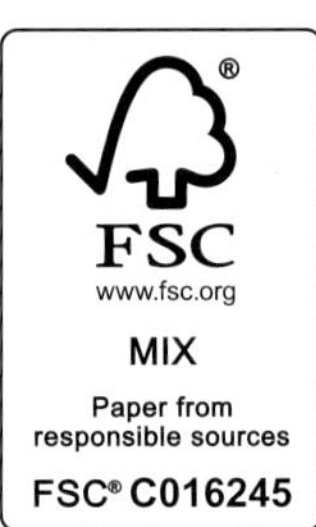

Library and Archives Canada Cataloguing in Publication

Stanbridge, Nicole, 1976-
    Throw down / Nicole Stanbridge, Wendy Welch.

Includes bibliographical references.
    Catalogue of the exhibition, Throw Down, held at the
    Art Gallery of Greater Victoria, Jan. 27 - May 6, 2012.
ISBN 978-0-88885-366-0

    1. Welch, Wendy, 1959- --Exhibitions. 2. Art Gallery of Greater Victoria--
Exhibitions. I. Welch, Wendy, 1959- II. Art Gallery of Greater Victoria III. Title.

N6549.W436A4 2012   709.2   C2011-907816-3

THROW DOWN

CONTENTS

INTRODUCTION/ INVITATION TO THROW DOWN

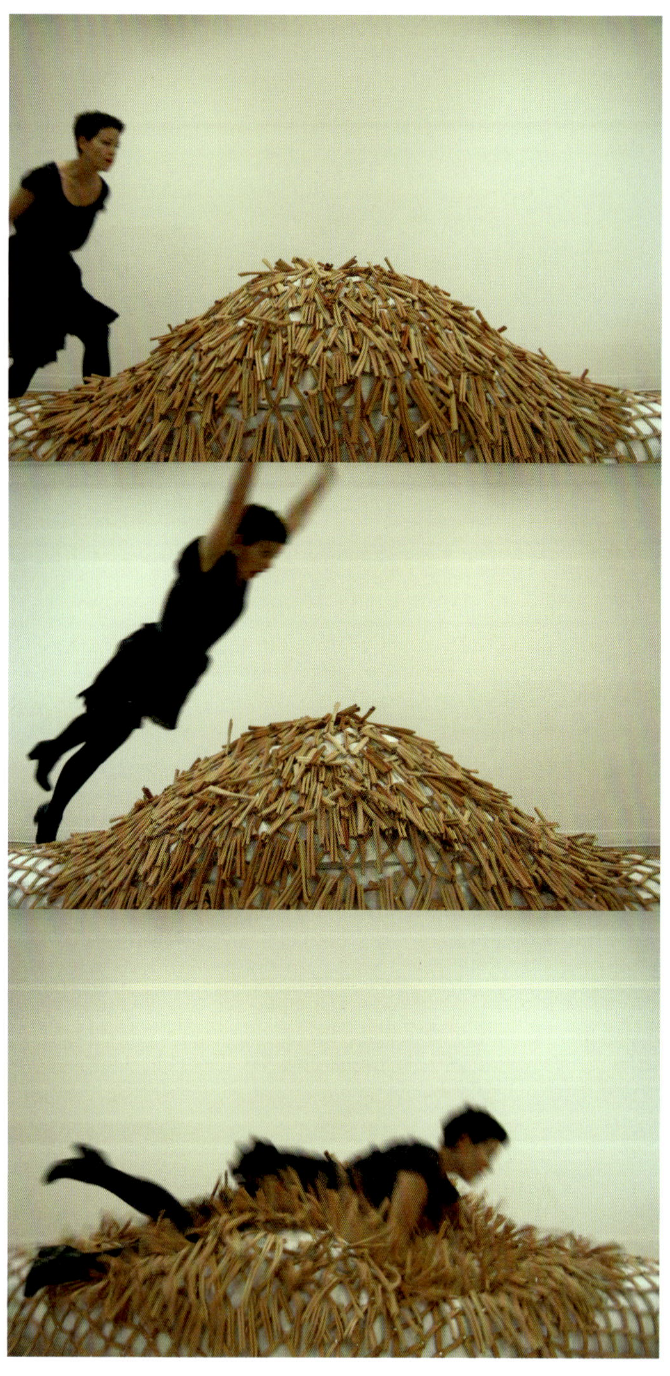

Megan Dickie | video stills, *Tussle with the Tangler*, 2012 | 4 channel video | dimensions variable | courtesy of the artist

To *throw down* can mean many things: to celebrate in a big way, to fight for something meaningful, to contribute resources to make things happen. These varied meanings are captured by the five artists from British Columbia who have been selected for this exhibition. Their use of sculpture, video, photography, drawing, and public intervention addresses socio-political and economic issues and employs strategies of satire and humour to articulate the celebration, the fight, and the desire to make things happen. The impetus for this publication and the exhibition was, first, to feature artists from British Columbia and celebrate the work they contribute to the discourse of contemporary art, offering a platform for the issues and ideals they promote through these bodies of work; and, second, to create a forum in which the current state of art production—its presentation and sustainability—could be discussed, specifically in relation to the current state of arts funding in British Columbia. In essence, it is the act of artists throwing down their livelihoods that is the driving force sustaining and supporting the visual arts.

THE STATE OF AFFAIRS

This exhibition provides a context in which we can assess the current lived reality for artists in British Columbia. In the wake of the economic downturn of 2008, arts funding took some big hits—$30 million had been cut from provincial funding to the arts by Fall 2009. While some of this support has been recovered, the impact of these cuts runs deep and has raised questions about the value of art in our society and how government policy reflects that value. It is telling to see what artists are throwing down in the way of personal resources, ideas, and time so they can continue to produce and present their art. And it is important to consider how artists, arts organizations, and funding bodies are navigating cuts to the arts in British Columbia.

Over the last three years the challenge has been to determine the exact status of arts funding in our province, a problem that began when gaming grants were frozen in August 2009. This grant program provided funding to charities and not-for-profit

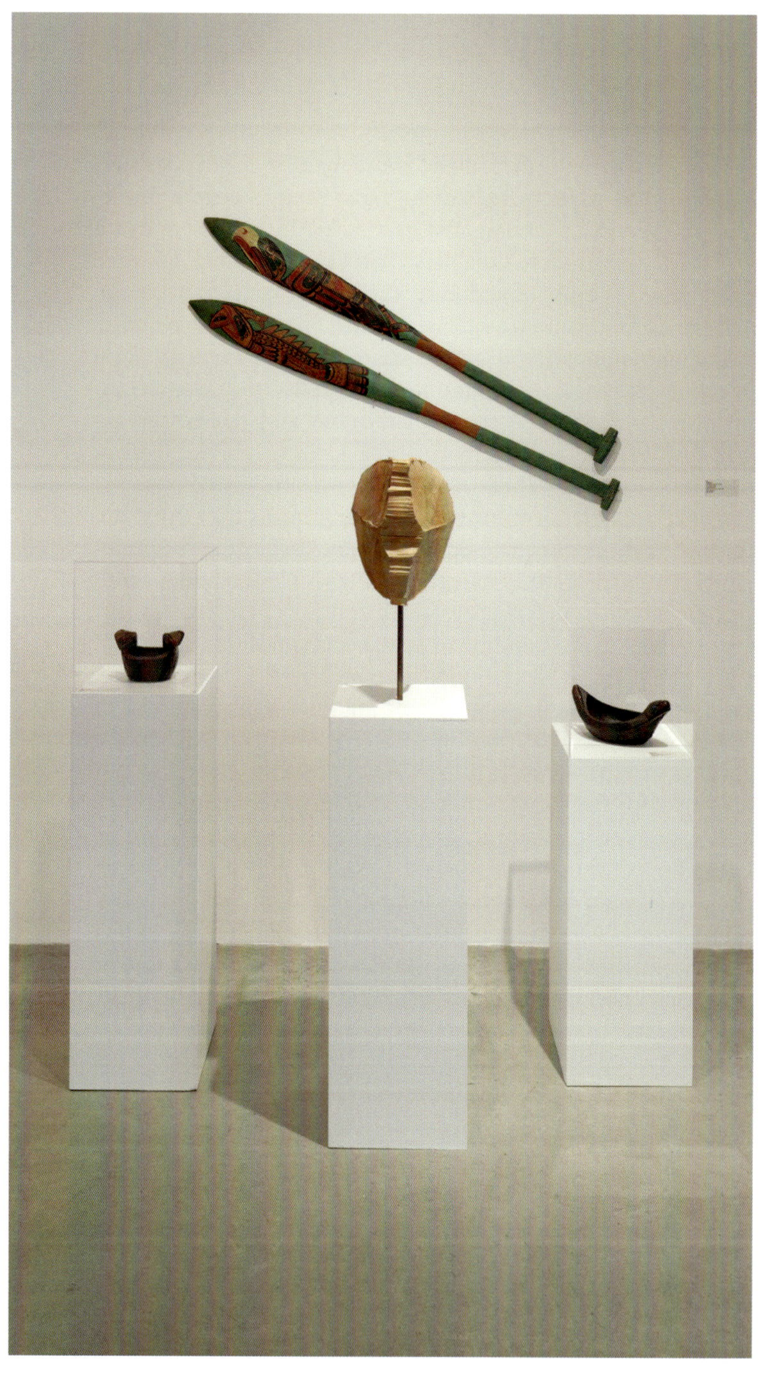

Sonny Assu and Eric Deis | *Equinox Gallery*, 2011 | archival pigment print | 71 x 106.5 cm | courtesy of the artists

organizations, and several of the groups in line to receive that funding were part of the arts and culture sector. In Fall 2009, arts communities in British Columbia took their concerns public, organizing rallies outside the provincial legislature and the offices of the BC Arts Council in Victoria to voice their concerns and address the impact of these cuts. Artists in other parts of the province also organized protests and educational events in their communities. While the government did restore portions of the funding over the next year, in November 2010 the BC Association for Charitable Gaming (BCCG), the group that represents the recipients of gaming grants, asked the provincial Auditor General to investigate the provincial government's administration and distribution of gaming proceeds transferred to it from the BC Lottery Corporation. On October 31, 2011, an independent review of gaming grant governance was submitted to the Ministry of Community, Sport and Cultural Development (which until September 2011 was known as the Ministry of Tourism, Culture and the Arts—note the omission of the word "art" in the new title).The results of this review are scheduled to be made public in January 2012.[1]

The gaming grants investigation occurred at the same time a change in provincial government leadership was taking place. During her successful campaign for the premiership, Christy Clark told an arts advocacy group that she would restore arts funding to 2008/09 levels.[2] However, Statistics Canada data show that British Columbia had the lowest level of federal and provincial arts funding per capita during those years.[3]

Given these statistics, what must artists themselves contribute to the infrastructure of the creative economy to support the production, delivery, promotion, and dissemination of ideas? The Art Gallery of York University (AGYU) polled the nation's artists to get an accurate picture of where they are, both economically and geographically. Based on the survey's results, the AGYU authors concluded that the arts make up a thriving viable sector, a point most people would agree with and support. However, what many may not be aware of is that "more than half of all visual artists (56%) lose money on their artistic practice...and pay a significant economic penalty to pursue their practice."[4] In other words, visual artists are the primary funders of their own artistic practices.[5]

This exhibition features a selection of artists who have chosen to stay in British Columbia and continue to support and contribute to the discourse on visual art in this province. They throw down not only for their careers as artists and their communities, but also for the survival of a creative workforce in the face of dire economic times. They wholeheartedly throw down for the viability of the art economy, make things happen in a big way, honour, promote, create, support, and celebrate with passion. The artists included in this project—Sonny Assu, Gregory Ball, Megan Dickie, Tyler Hodgins, Alison MacTaggart, contributing writer Wendy Welch, and catalogue designer Ross Macaulay— all give back to their communities in diverse ways as artists and, in many cases, as educators, administrators, promoters, and writers. The work selected for the exhibition speaks specifically to issues and ideals that are relevant to each of the artists. Through humour, satire, and critique, the act of throwing down extends into issues of identity, value, preservation, social injustice, consumption, and play.

The themes in Megan Dickie's new sculptural work *Submission*, and the related video work *Step into the Ring*, were the impetus for this exhibition and its exploration of the act of throwing down. Her adult-scale bop-bag (the toy that, after you've punched it, pops back up to meet you for another round) in the shape of the Canada Council logo speaks dynamically to the shared challenges faced by artists, institutions, and funding agencies to keep art thriving. This work literally illustrates the artist's attempt to wrestle this icon of funding into submission—to fight and not submit or be dissuaded by the struggle. Fighting, or wrestling, has informed Dickie's ongoing series *Contact Games*. These works invite play and physicality as a means of exposing the human tendency to indulge in spectacle. Roland Barthes articulated this desire in his essay "The World of Wrestling,"

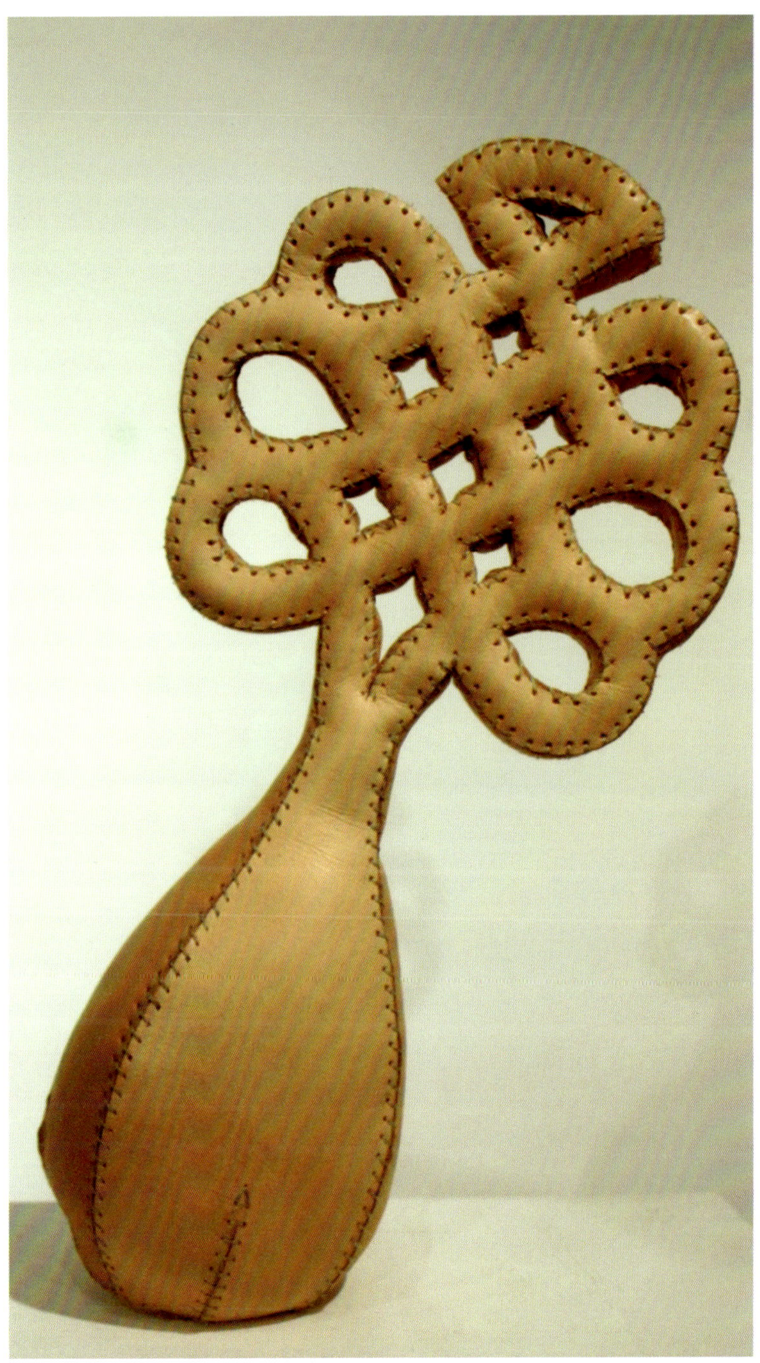

Megan Dickie | *Submission,* maquette, 2009 | leather, polyester filling, sand | 17.5 x 12.5 x 35.5 cm | courtesy of the artist

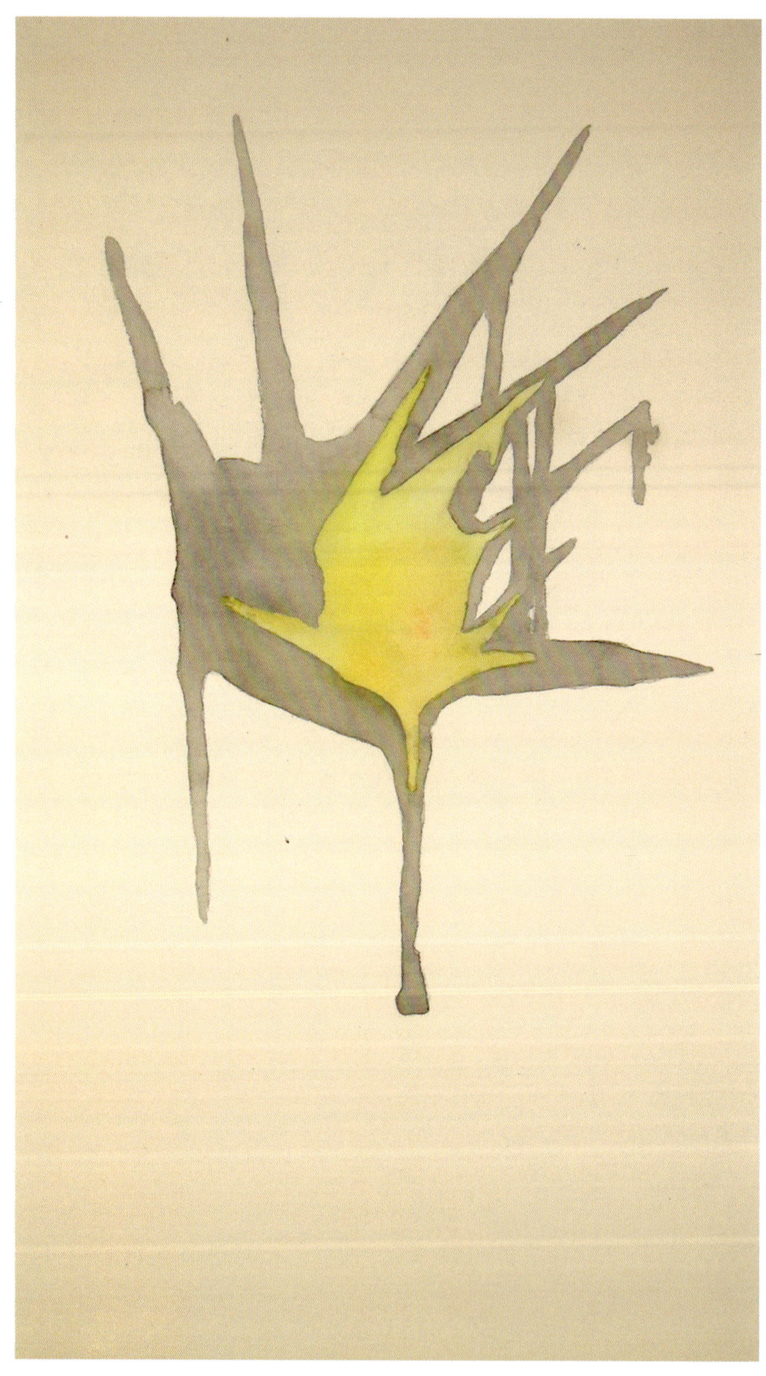

Alison MacTaggart | detail, *The Egg Throwing Apparatus*, 2002 | wood, hardware
watercolour on paper | dimensions variable | courtesy of the artist

in which he discussed the transparency of the constructed spectacle (wrestling), and our willingness to make the leap to engage with it and have it evoke a real emotional response in spite of its artifice.[6] Dickie's intention in highlighting physicality through her work is to "break down the hierarchy that exists between physical and mental states by engaging with an object on a tactile level before the censorship of reason kicks in."[7]

Although we inherently place more value on truthful things, we suspend that need for reality when we indulge in guilty pleasures. Dickie's sculptures and Tyler Hodgins' wall installation *Please Try Again* both employ repetitive gestures to address the notion that we are willing to disregard our good sense in order to engage in play. In this piece, Hodgins creates a grid of used crossword scratch-and-win tickets that have, in fact, lost. The repetition of scratching and losing, and the repetition of words and patterns that emerge, creates an aesthetically engaging work with changing hues and pattern. Of particular interest to Hodgins "is the filtering of a popular and recognizable form of entertainment through a visual compulsion to order and build objects, as well as the slow accumulation of meaning through repetitive acts."[8]

Like Megan Dickie, Alison MacTaggart uses elements of design and invention in her sculptures to tease our curiosity and lead us to investigate larger ideas of human impulse. The structure of these artists' forms invites tactile or imagined tactile responses, which Dickie uses to expose the moments of indulgence we impulsively entertain, turning "intellectual breakthroughs into novelty gadgets or absurd props for comic relief."[9] Similarly, MacTaggart's *The Egg Throwing Apparatus* appears to be a self-explanatory functional gadget for the act of egg throwing. The results of its actions are illustrated by abstract watercolours on the wall that suggest a smashed egg, explosions, and nerve cells. While we do not witness the function of the apparatus, MacTaggart engages us visually so we can imagine the intended action. The appeal of interactive objects is their potential to perform, although Jean Baudrillard sees gadgets as existing in "a whole world of functional delusion...in which a role is played by irrational complexity, obsessive detail, eccentric technicity or gratuitous formalism."[10] It is the materiality, interaction, and didactic nature of gadgets that appeals to our compulsion to imagine their potential. Even if that potential is only in theory or small in impact, we derive pleasure from the exercise. For MacTaggart, *The Egg Throwing Apparatus* has a greater potential role then just the imagined gesture. This work is a way for her to address what happens when individuals identify themselves to their community as queer. They are called out and named publicly, which makes them visible, but also puts them at risk. MacTaggart uses humour to disarm the metaphorical egg throwing that could occur as a result of intolerance and discrimination.

Sonny Assu's contribution to the exhibition includes a new body of work that is a departure from, and a progressive evolution in, his already diverse practice. Earlier works referenced and challenged popular consumer culture and traditional aboriginal forms through painting, sculpture, and installation; this new series, however, is the first time he has worked with found objects. He has taken cuts of cedar from a log home development on the We Wei Kai Nation reserve in Campbell River, BC, where his family lives. With no alterations made to them, these objects, which had been discarded as refuse, take on new meaning and purpose. Although they remain faceless, they appear to be longing for identity as traditional First Nation masks, in contrast to the artifacts and artwork with which they come to share space. Assu has created mounts for the "masks," which transport them into an institutional context as objects for display. Assu saw parallels in the loss of First Nations culture through colonization and subsequent policies and infrastructures that were put in place to suppress aboriginal traditions.

Also included in this series are photographed portraits of these masks, isolating them as artifacts, and documentation of them as interventions in the series *Artifacts of Authenticity*, a collaboration with artist Eric Deis. The photo-documentation presents the masks in situ as interventions in the context of a museum (artifact), commercial gallery (fine art), and gift shop (souvenir).

The objects take on many layers of meaning for Assu. As a material or resource, the cedar cuts raise questions about how we assign value in society. To the log home developers, these remnants of cedar were refuse. Because of the diversity of uses for cedar in First Nations tradition, however, Assu was able to find meaning and value in the material and its inadvertent reference to Northwest Coast masks. As interventions within spaces of meaning creation (i.e., the museum, commercial gallery, or gift shop), the masks bring into question the self-imposed/self-assigned authority of those spaces to define what and who qualifies as aboriginal.

The placement of these works as interventions changes their context, an effect we also see in Tyler Hodgins' new commission *Sleeping Bag*. Depending on where the work is placed, it creates a conversation with its environment and confronts us in spaces and ways we do not anticipate. With *Sleeping Bag*, Hodgins has created a series of temporal sculptural interventions that take place throughout the city of Victoria during the run of the *Throw Down* exhibition. The sculptures are cast forms of figures in a sleeping bag, made of coloured ice and placed in various locations throughout the city centre, to be encountered by people in their daily routines. Over time the forms will melt, leaving only a trace of colour from the ice, which will eventually wash away with exposure to the elements. Their ephemeral nature speaks to the lack of visibility of the homeless and the lack of action taken to address issues of homelessness. Hodgins' motivation was to draw the "public gaze towards a public problem," which is a poignant reminder in many ways of our societal failings. Like Assu, Hodgins in some ways departs from his previous practice with this work. He has completed several permanent public commissions throughout the city, including *Rings* (2007) at the Lochside trailhead in Saanich, *Topography* (2007) at the Burnside-Gorge Community Centre, and *Glass Half Full* (2011) at Holland Point Park on Dallas Road. These works suggest ideas of community, history, memory, play, interaction, and form; in contrast, this new work has a very clear and provocative purpose: to direct our focus, if only for a moment, to the prevalent issue of homelessness in our city.

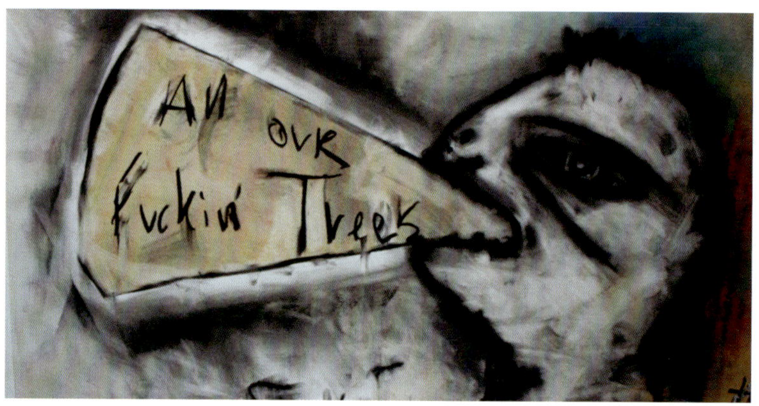

Gregory Ball | video still, *You Suck!*, 2009/2012 | video installation, drawings | dimensions variable | courtesy of the artist

Gregory Ball's work *You Suck!* is also a provocation, shaking us out of our complacency. Consisting of a video installation and a series of drawings, the work references natural landscape, industrial practices, and consumer culture. The main character in his animation, a foul-mouthed, ranting talking head, adds an element of humour to the otherwise intense moral outcry for environmental awareness and social consciousness. The imagery in Ball's work spools from an accumulation of sources: dreams, media/popular culture, and, more generally, the everyday. He finds himself engrossed with this rendering of the "odd" details in life. The new installation component of this work—an oil drum scored and beaten with images and language from the animation—refers to a primitive zoetrope (a device that produces an illusion of action from a rapid succession of static pictures). The inclusion of the oil drum was inspired by a recent act of solidarity with his colleagues. During the 2011 strike at Vancouver Island University, a convening area formed around an oil drum in which wood was burned to keep the striking employees warm. What evolved at this meeting place was the sharing of collective stories and opportunities for meaningful dialogue. While the statement expressed in the title of this work might appear to be an act of aggression, the real intent is a call to action.

The essay contribution by Wendy Welch, *Does the World Need Another Art School?* (to which her answer is a resounding "Yes"), articulates the personal investment required to make things happen in a big way in the arts sector. Welch's life and work as artist, art writer, curator, and educator, as well as the founder and director of the Vancouver Island School of Art, embody the act of throwing down. She has devised a way to navigate the hurdles imposed on the arts sector by constructing resources and opportunities on her own terms. The challenge inspires and encourages her to create an environment that provides an open exchange of ideas and makes contemporary art practices accessible for all people.

While there may not be immediate answers to or resolution of the state of art funding and production in British Columbia, opening up dialogue and discussion on the topic can instigate change. The art sector is known for its creative problem solving, its ability to throw down and succeed in the face of adversity. If we can honour that spirit and use it as a resource, perhaps solutions will appear—or at least we will increase awareness that art is relevant and crucial to the well-being of society.

Nicole Stanbridge
November 2011

1. See Province of BC, Community Gaming Grant Review website, http://www.communitygaminggrantreview.gov.bc.ca/.

2. Jessica Werb, "Christy Clark says she'll restore arts funding," Straight.com, February 10, 2011, http://www.straight.com/article-374240/vancouver/christy-clark-says-shell-restore-arts-funding.

3. See "Government expenditures on culture in 2008/09," *Arts Research Monitor* 10, no. 1 (July 2011), an analysis of Statistics Canada, "Government Expenditures on Culture: Data Tables, 2008/2009," http://www.statcan.gc.ca/pub/87f0001x/87f0001x2011001-eng.htm?WT.mc_id=twtB0869?WT.mc_id=twtB0868.

4. Michael Maranda, *Waging Culture: The socio-economic status of Canadian visual artists* (Toronto: Art Gallery of York University, 2009), http://theagyuisoutthere.org/everywhere/?p=1443.

5. According to the AGYU study: "Artists pay a significant economic penalty to pursue their practice, and are, through real monetary contributions, replacing potential income-earning employment with what amounts to free labour. In 2007, the average artist worked 26 hours per week on their studio practice, 14.5 hours on art-related employment, and 7.6 hours on non-art-related employment. In addition, they volunteered just over 3 hours a week to art-related activities. Those artists who spent a majority of their employment time in the studio earned significantly less total income, a median of $15,000, versus $28,994 for artists who spent most of their time in art-related employment, and $21,793 for those who spent most of their time in non-art-related employment."

6. Roland Barthes, "The World of wrestling," http://www9.georgetown.edu/faculty/irvinem/theory/Barthes-Mythologies-Wrestling-1957.pdf.

7. Megan Dickie, artist statement, http://megandickie.com/projects-contact-games-sculptures/.

8. Tyler Hodgins, artist statement, http://www.tylerhodgins.ca/studio?itemid=14.

9. Megan Dickie, artist statement, http://megandickie.com/projects-contact-games-sculptures/.

10. Jean Baudrillard, *The System of Objects*, trans. James Benedict (London: Verso, 2005), p. 121. First published as *Le systéme des object* (Paris: Gallimard, 1968).

DOES THE WORLD NEED ANOTHER ART SCHOOL?

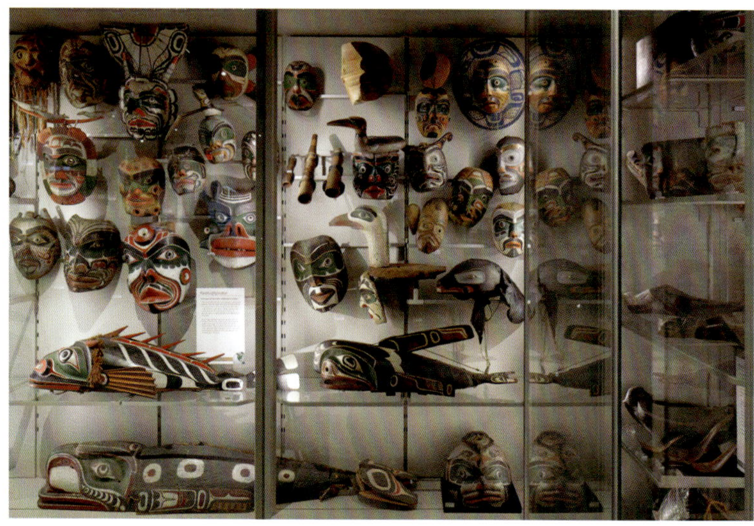

Sonny Assu and Eric Deis | *Museum of Anthropology*, 2011 | archival pigment print | 71 x 106.5 cm | courtesy of the artists

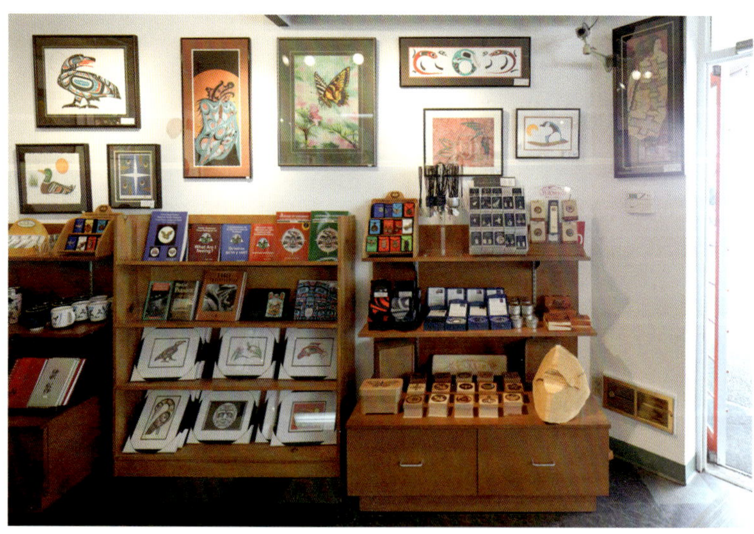

Sonny Assu and Eric Deis | *Roberts Gallery and Gifts*, 2011 | archival pigment print | 71 x 106.5 cm | courtesy of the artists

WHEN I was studying art at university, the first session of each course would begin with an announcement from the professor: "Only one percent of you are going to make it as artists." A dismal statistic considering we were usually at least 25 students in a class, and most people in the room were thinking that making it as an artist was the whole purpose of their education. I have come to learn that an education in the arts is about so much more than that end goal of becoming an artist.

Several years ago, in a casual conversation with a former director of the Art Gallery of Greater Victoria about teaching art, the question came up: "Why would you want to be in the business of creating more artists? Isn't the world already oversaturated with art and the people who make it?" My response was, "The job of the art school isn't only about making future artists. It is to teach visual literacy and an appreciation for the role art plays in the development and understanding of who we are as human beings, as well as to create future supporters of the art gallery." He smiled at that last part.

When I first mentioned the idea of starting an art school, the general response from people was disbelief and confusion. My initial motive was self-serving: I wanted to create an interesting job for myself. In a recent interview, Rirkrit Tiravanija said, "Artists are understanding that they can be the center of what they are interested in. They don't have to go to the center. They can make their own terms. The information or discussion will reach out."[1] Another side goal was that I wanted to form a group of interesting artists to hang out with on a regular basis. When I completed my MFA in 2003, I found myself confronting two choices: I could continue to seek out a "placement" for myself somewhere in the university system across Canada (the usual post-MFA route) or I could create my own position and get to choose my workplace colleagues. The second choice was much more seductive. As Roland Barthes said: "There is only one way left to escape the alienation of present day society—*to retreat ahead of it.*"[2] The Vancouver Island School of Art (VISA) was established in 2004.

Victoria is a conservative city at the edge of the country. This is a place that isn't exactly receptive to contemporary art (the ongoing outrage at Mowry Baden's public art sculptures is testament to this). I knew starting a contemporary art school would not be an easy business venture to take on here—or probably anywhere else, for that matter. I knew we would have to offer something unique to give people a reason to choose our school over the other art education options in the city, including university and college programs and the numerous art courses offered at recreation centres. VISA was founded on the idea that we could be everything to everybody: friendly, accessible, contemporary, adventurous, student-focused, and community-focused. On top of all that, we also insisted on offering a high-quality, rigorous curriculum (we recently achieved an articulation agreement with Emily Carr University, which means our one-year Certificate of Visual Arts is transferable to the first year of a BFA degree). Having "friendly" at the beginning of the list made everything else that followed possible.

The recent Hollywood film *Moneyball* (2011) shows how Billy Beane, the general manager of the Oakland A's baseball team, learned to make an underdog team succeed: focus on the idiosyncrasies that make you stand out from the others and work from there. As a "small player" (a non-funded private art school) working amongst the "big players" (university and college art programs), VISA risks losing its qualified faculty to the well-funded institutions that can pay them more. Rather than admit defeat and submit to this reality, we factor in this changing and diverse faculty as an opportunity to continually reinvent ourselves. In turn, this keeps the school alive and dynamic.

Another asset we have is our location: we are just outside the downtown perimeter. Often the only people who go to university or college art departments are students and instructors. At VISA, everybody comes through our doors: people on their way to work or on their way home from the grocery store; people walking their dogs or getting their morning coffee. Our doors are always open. The only way we can compete in the game is

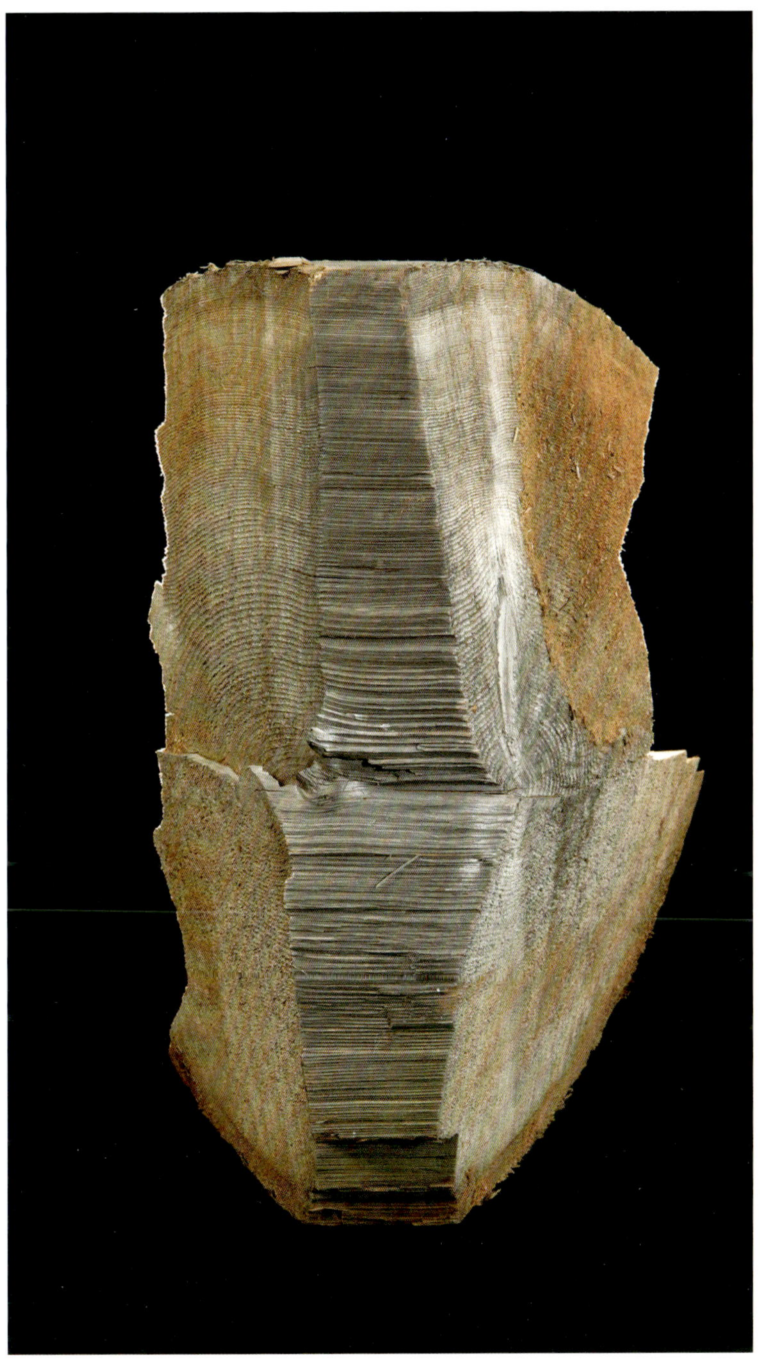

Sonny Assu | *Wise Ones (Elder #4)*, 2011 | archival pigment print | 38 x 49 cm |
courtesy of the artist and Equinox Gallery

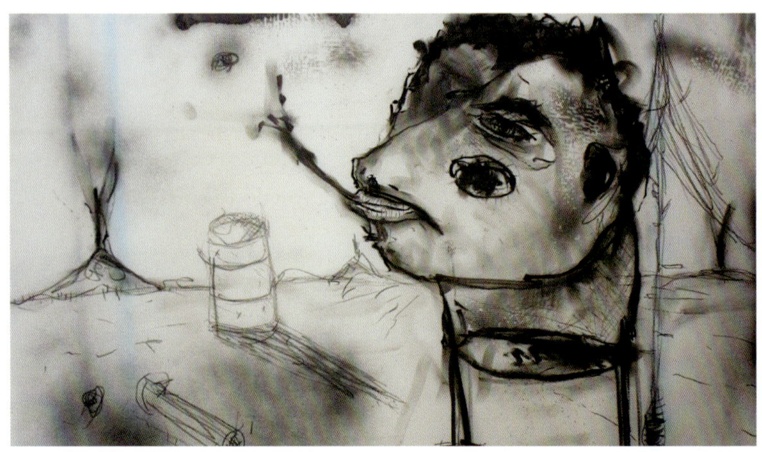

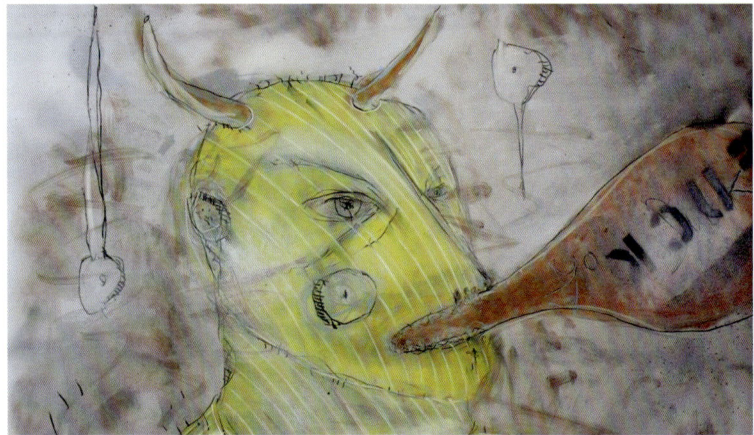

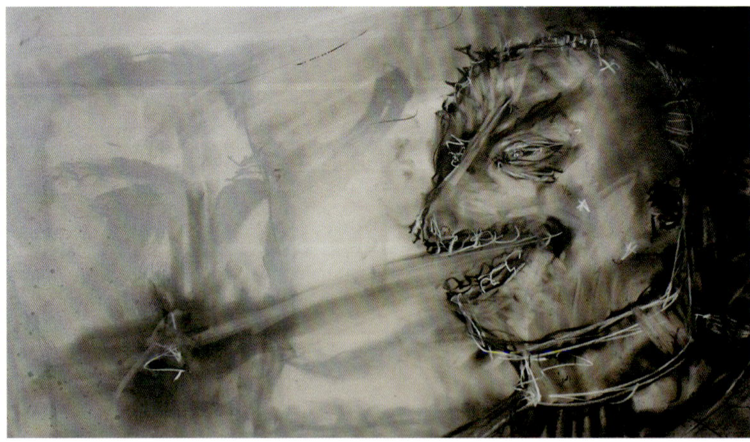

Gregory Ball | drawings from *You Suck!*, 2012 | video installation, drawings, mixed media on vellum | dimensions variable | courtesy of the artist

by being distinctly different. In the words of Billy Beane, "The pleasure of rooting for Goliath is that you can expect to win. The pleasure of rooting for David is that, while you don't know what to expect, you stand at least a chance of being inspired."[3]

Art changes the way we see and interpret the world. Dr Joel Katz of Harvard Medical School conducts an art course in which medical students study artworks in the Boston Museum of Fine Arts. In July 2008 the *Boston Globe* reported: "Katz's belief that physicians can improve their diagnostic skills by observing art was bolstered this month when he and his colleagues published a study in the Journal of General Internal Medicine showing that after completing the class, students' ability to make accurate observations increased 38 percent."[4] The Frick Museum in New York offers art courses for police officers and FBI agents to help them enhance their powers of observation.[5] These examples illustrate the use of art education beyond the simple end goal of producing an endless stream of professional artists. The art school exists to enable people to be more creative, observant, and engaged.

Instructional classes are only one component of the educational activities at VISA. Other activities include exhibitions in the Slide Room Gallery; collaborative community works such as the Crystal Pool Mural; projects in our backyard, including a graffiti wall, temporary sculpture installations (such as *Watch This Space* by Tyler Hodgins), a herb garden (*The People's Apothecary*, to be launched in spring 2012), and our Garry oak meadow (started in 2006 as an homage to Joseph Beuys' *7000 Oaks*). In addition, we have an ongoing series of artist talks, open studio drop-in, and music events, and we work with local theatre companies, such as Theatre Skam and the Fringe Festival. All these activities add to the distinct nature of our major role: art school as community organization.

Jay Coogan, in *Rethinking the Contemporary Art School*, sums up the philosophy of VISA: "The value that art schools bring to the culture is that they create an environment that promotes creative thinking. To offer a valued educational environment, we need to

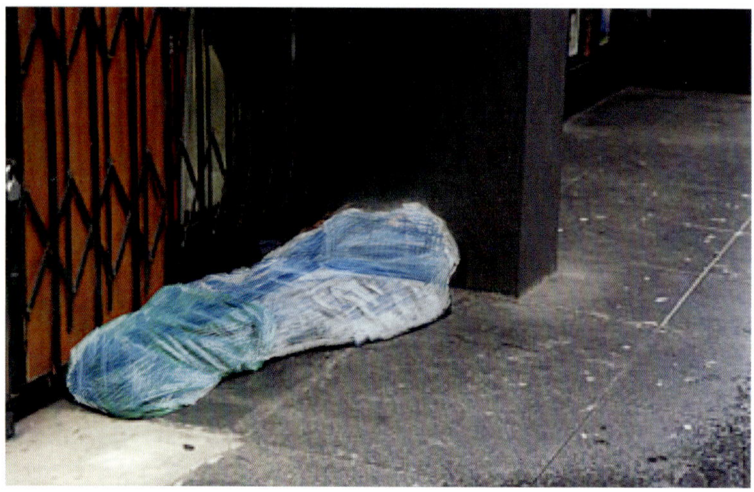

Tyler Hodgins | *Sleeping Bag,* concept drawing, 2011 | courtesy of the artist

ensure that it will continue to have meaning and purpose and to attract an energetic community of students and faculty. To assist in developing the creative process, we need instructors who will model open and collaborative vision. We must nurture students so that they are able to confront challenges and discover new ways of being, and by doing so, continue to evolve culture."[6] Art education is more than instruction on how to draw, paint, or take photographs. Art education connects the individual to the community at both a local and global level; it gives agency to individuals to construct contemporary culture and it increases perception and awareness resulting in a more complex world-view. Art education makes Socrates' idea of an examined life possible.

As a visual artist who engages in installation art and relies on collaboration with others to assemble my work in gallery spaces, I often find myself slipping seamlessly between my roles of artist and executive director of an art school. The art school resembles a contemporary art project at times, especially in terms of working with the faculty to develop an exciting curriculum and then seeing this acted out through the teaching of classes. The work of Rirkrit Tiravanija comes to mind when I think about this process. Tiravanija's practive involves gathering an audience together in a gallery space and serving them food. Amy Stafford describes Rirkrit's work: "While others have come before in challenging this fundamental art world paradigm, Rirkrit Tiravanija is driven not so much by political agenda but more simply the impetus to encourage his audience to get down with the art and become an integral part of it in the process. His work dissolves the tenuous boundaries between viewer and participant, inviting the audience to interact, engage and enjoy—as if it weren't a formal exhibition at all, but a gathering of friends, sharing stories and temporarily escaping the pervasively isolated nature of contemporary life."[7] I see the art school as a meeting place where members of the community, ranging in age from 18 to 80, from all rungs of the social-economic ladder and every cultural background, can come together to discuss ideas about contemporary art and culture.

> Is school a place, an institution, a set of facilities, a situation, a circumstance, an attitude, or a constellation of relationships for the transfer of acquired, invented, and accumulated knowledge, experience, and insight from one generation to another? Perhaps a school or the idea of a school as a condition of learning, of being open to discourse and discovery, can also be seen as something that we might carry with us wherever we go, whatever we do.[8]

If an art school is any or all of these things, then, yes, the world needs more of them.

Wendy Welch
November 2011

1. From an interview done during Rirkrit Tiravanija's on-site preparation for 21st Century: Art in the First Decade at the Gallery of Modern Art (GoMA) in Brisbane, Australia, from December 18, 2010, to April 26, 2011. Tiravanija spoke with Russell Storer, curatorial manager Asian and Pacific Art, about his practice.

2. Roland Barthes, *The Pleasure of the Text* (New York: Hill and Wang, 1975), p. 40.

3. Michael Lewis, *Moneyball: The Art of Winning an Unfair Game* (New York: WW Norton, 2003), p. 115.

4. Liz Kowalczyk, "Monet? Gauguin? Using art to make better doctors: New courses improve powers of observation," *Boston Globe*, July 20, 2008.

5. Neal Hirschfield, "Teaching cops to see at New York City's Metropolitan Museum of Art, Amy Herman schools police in the fine art of deductive observation," *Smithsonian Magazine*, October 2009.

6. Jay Coogan, "Evolutionary forces: Advancing art and design education," in *Rethinking the Contemporary Art School: The Artist, the PhD, and the Academy*, ed. Brad Buckley and John Conomos (Halifax: NSCAD Press, 2009), p. 125.

7. Amy Stafford, "Rirkrit Tiravanija," *Surface Magazine* 15, November 1998.

8. Raqs Media Collective, "How to be an artist by night," in *Art School* (*Propositions for the 21st Century*), ed. Steven Henry Madoff (Cambridge, MA: MIT Press, 2009), p. 74.

ARTISTS' BIOGRAPHIES

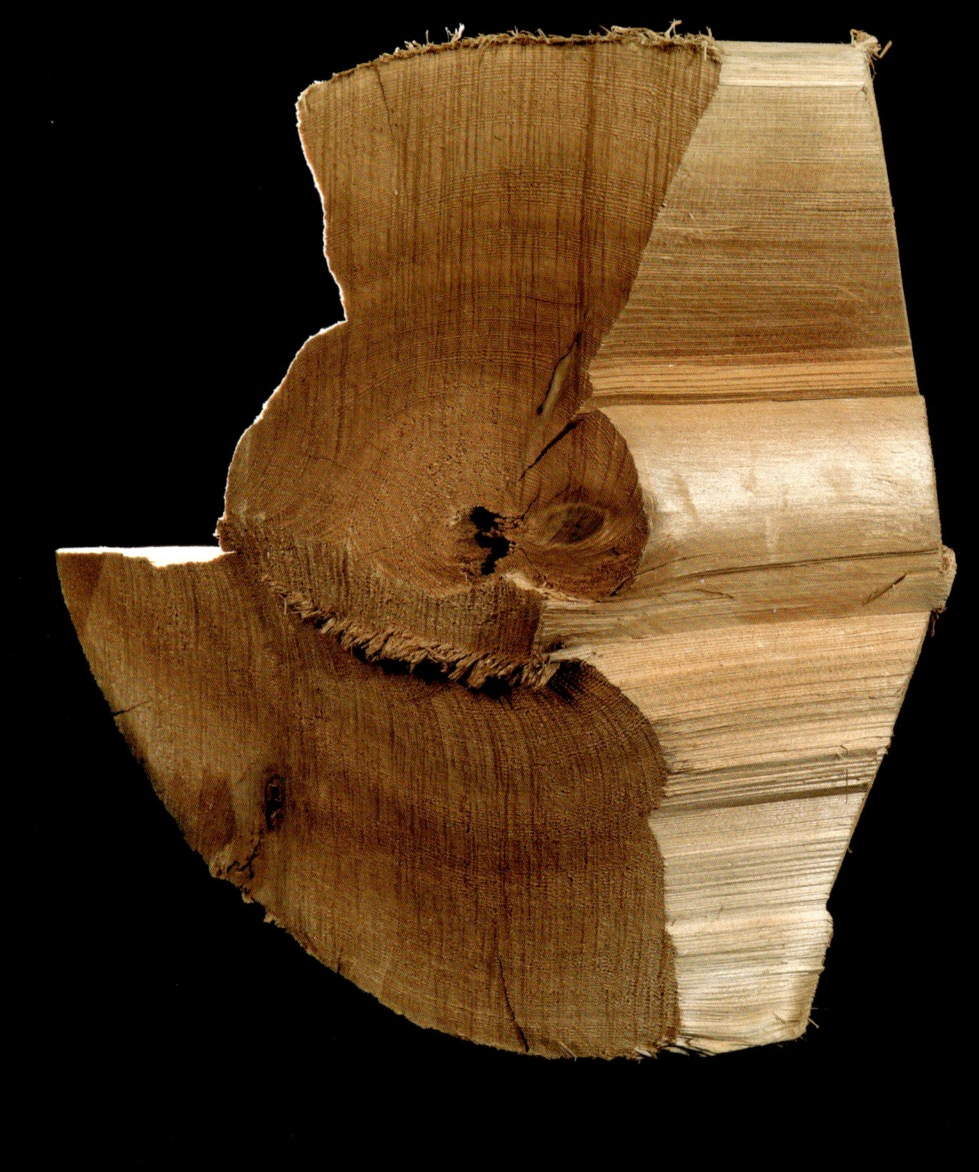

ONNY ASSU, formerly a Vancouver-based artist, is now living and working in Montreal, QC. Assu is Laich-kwil-tach (Kwakwaka'wakw) of the We Wai Kai First Nation (Cape Mudge). He received his BFA from Emily Carr College of Art and Design (now Emily Carr University) in 2002 with a focus on print media, painting, and digital arts. He has been awarded several grants from the Canada Council for the Arts and the British Columbia Arts Council, beginning in 2004. Most recently he received the BC Creative Achievement Award for First Nations Art. Selections of his works are in the collections of the National Gallery of Canada, the Museum of Anthropology at the University of British Columbia, the City of Richmond's Olympic Oval, and the Seattle Art Museum. Assu's work has been exhibited in numerous solo and group shows across Canada and the United States since 2002; recent exhibitions include Longing (West Vancouver Museum, West Vancouver, BC, 2011), Silenced (Equinox Gallery, Vancouver, BC, 2011), Decolonize Me (Ottawa Art Gallery, Ottawa, ON, 2011), Don't Stop Me Now! (National Gallery of Canada, Ottawa, Ont, 2011), Sonny Assu (Equinox Gallery, Vancouver, BC, 2010, and 2008), Alternorthern (The Lab, San Francisco, CA, 2010), Blue Like an Orange (Ottawa Art Gallery, Ottawa, ON, 2009), How Soon Is Now? (Vancouver Art Gallery, Vancouver, BC, 2009), iDrums (Equinox Gallery, Gallery 2, Vancouver, BC, 2009), and iPotlatch (Art Gallery of South Western Manitoba, Brandon, MB, 2007), among several others.

Assu continues to push the boundaries of contemporary art by challenging the perception of aboriginal art, merging aboriginal iconography with the aesthetics of popular culture in order to question the social and historical values placed upon both. An exploration of his mixed ancestry, his work appropriates or transforms items of consumer and popular culture to trace the lineage of his own life. Assu is interested in ideas surrounding aboriginal issues, branding, and new technologies. He works across many boundaries and disciplines, and in doing so reveals a ravishing oeuvre that speaks to many.

Sonny Assu | *We Wai Kai (Warrior #1)*, 2011 | archival pigment print | 38 x 49 cm | courtesy of the artist and Equinox Gallery

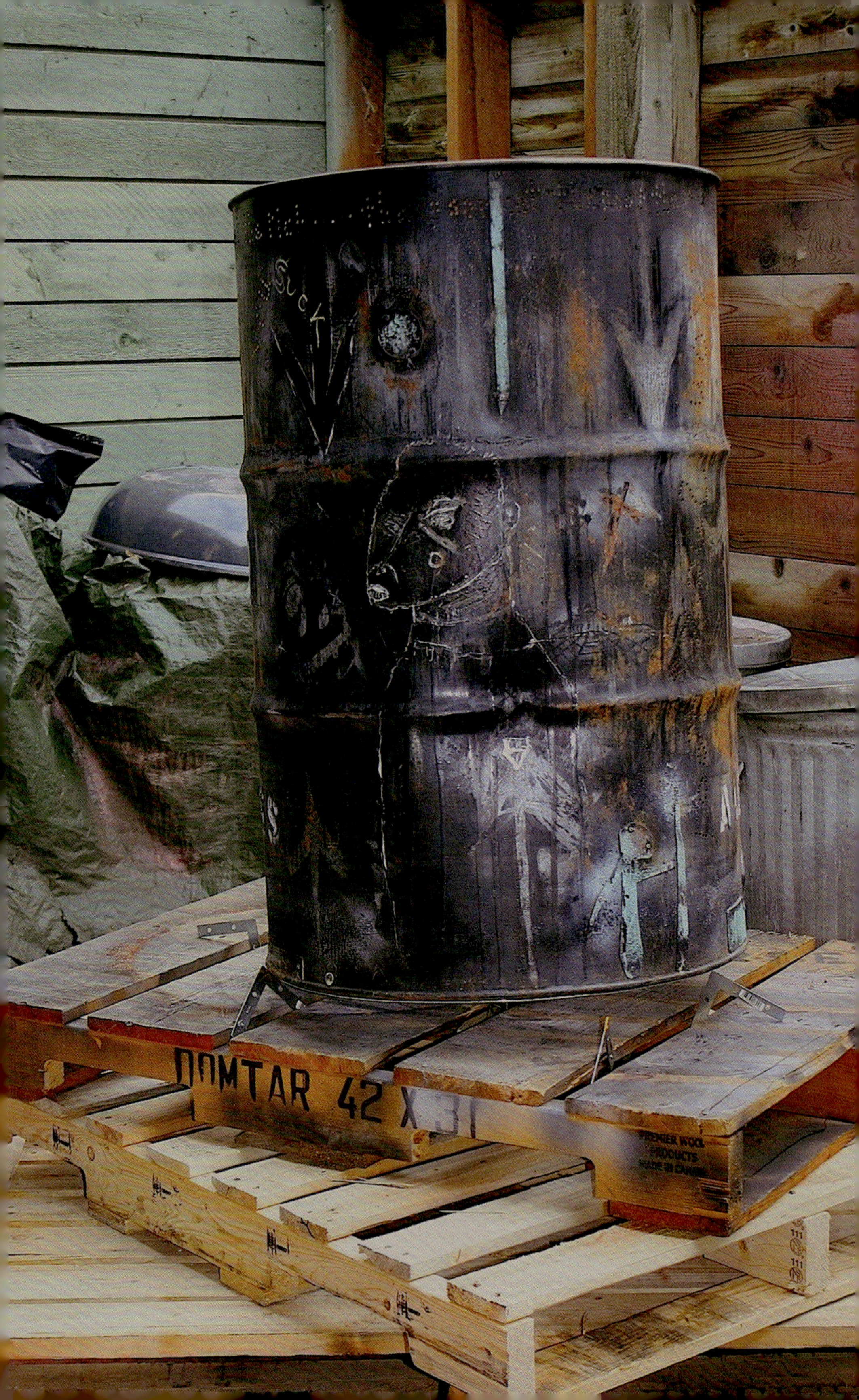

DOMTAR 42 X 31
PREMIER WOOL
PRODUCTS
MADE IN CANADA

GREGORY BALL is a Ladysmith-based artist, educator, and curator. Born and raised in Victoria, BC, he pursued formal training in visual arts, completing the Visual Art program at Camosun College in Victoria in 1984. Ball graduated with an honours degree in drawing and painting from Emily Carr College of Art and Design in 1986. In May of that year he moved to Toronto, ON, and became a working member of Open Studio printmaking centre. In 1989 he was accepted into the Banff Centre's artist-in-residence program, where he was inspired and mentored by artist and studio head Greg Curnoe. After a year at the Banff Centre, Ball moved to Montreal, QC, and embarked on a graduate degree in printmaking at Concordia University, where he graduated in 1994. He returned to Vancouver Island in 1995, and in 1999 accepted a position in the Visual Arts Department at Malaspina University College (now Vancouver Island University) in Nanaimo, BC. Ball continues to teach in the areas of drawing and printmaking. In addition to his teaching duties, he has held additional administrative positions such as curator of the Nanaimo Art Gallery, chair of the Visual Arts Department, and art and design club liaison and New York trip coordinator. Recent exhibitions include projects at Haida Gwaii Museum and the Comox Art Gallery.

Ball's work addresses issues related to the environment/landscape and the imbalance of power structures inherent in our society.

Gregory Ball | *You Suck!*, new work in progress, 2009/2012 | oil drum, mixed media | courtesy of the artist

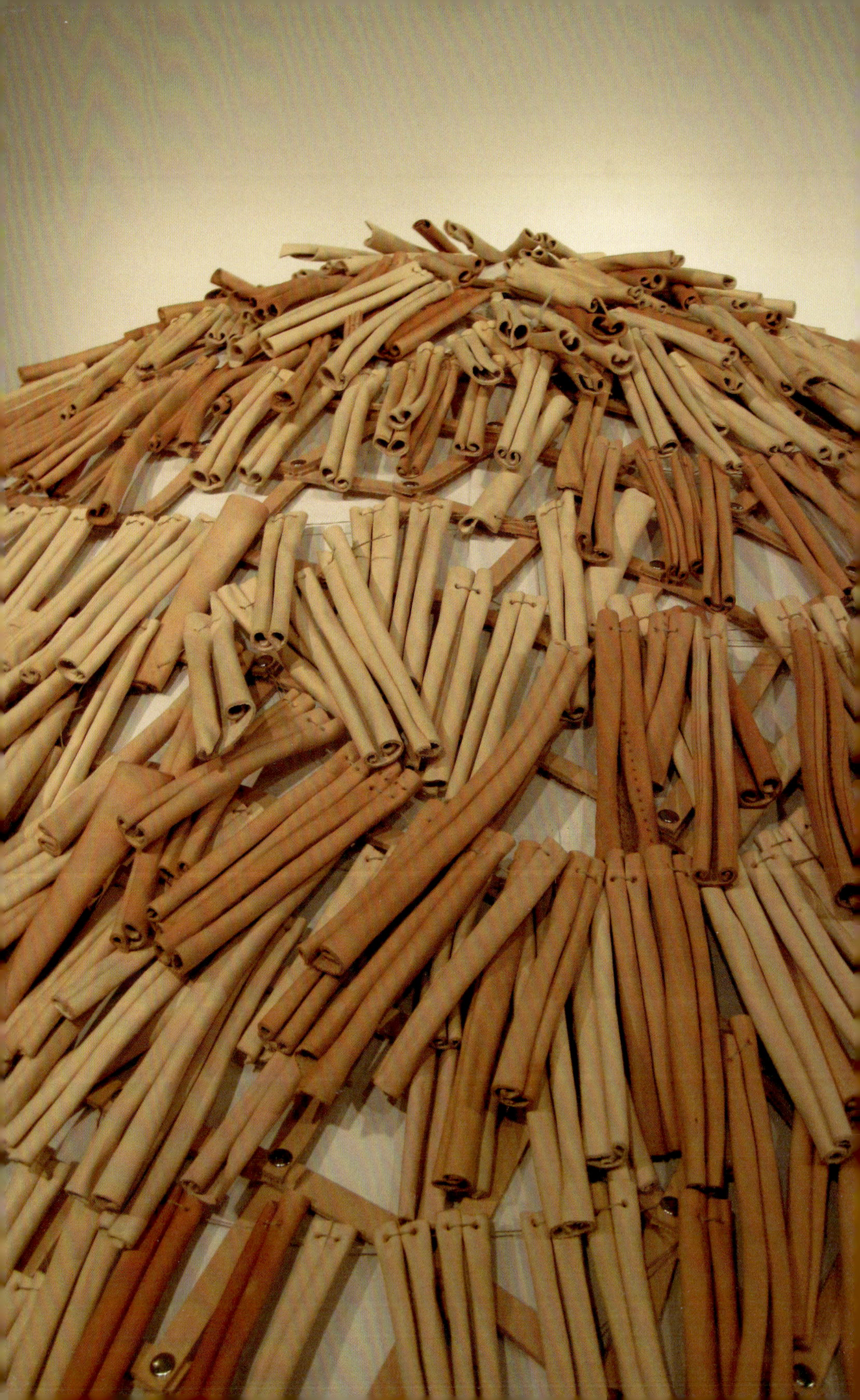

MEGAN DICKIE is a Victoria-based sculptor, printmaker, and educator. She completed a BFA in printmaking at the University of Calgary in 1997 before concluding her MFA in sculpture at the University of Saskatchewan, 2002. She was awarded two Project Assistance grants from the BC Arts Council in 2006 and 2008, as well as the Canada Council for the Arts Emerging Artist Creation/Production grant in 2004. Select artworks from Dickie's portfolio are in the permanent collections of the Nickel Arts Museum, the Alberta Foundation for the Arts, and the University of Saskatchewan. Dickie's artworks have been exhibited in various solo and group shows, including Get the Gleamer (Stride Gallery, Calgary, AB, 2012), Title TBA, with Diana Burgoyne (Touchstones Nelson: Museum of Art and History, Nelson, BC, 2012), Contact Games (Deluge Contemporary Art, Victoria, BC, 2010), Ready to Rumble (Ministry of Casual Living, Victoria, BC, 2009), Multitasker (The LAB 5.3, Art Gallery of Greater Victoria, Victoria, BC, 2005), This Train: Fine Arts Alumni 1990-2010 (Kenderdine Gallery, Saskatoon, SK, 2008, 2010), CAG Auction (Contemporary Art Gallery, Vancouver, BC, 2010), Push Pull (Art Produce, San Diego, CA, 2008), Fusible Link (PIP Gallery, Portland, OR, 2008), among numerous others. Dickie currently works as a sessional instructor of printmaking, sculpture, and drawing in the Department of Visual Arts at the University of Victoria.

Her work is both interactive and performative, at times privileging amusement over reason. Her recent projects highlight her continued use of functional forms and their ultimate transformation into exaggerated novelty gadgets. Inspired by complex design structures, like those of inventor and theorist Buckminster Fuller, Dickie's work is rigorous in form yet impulsive in function.

Megan Dickie | detail, *The Tangler*, 2010 | leather, vinyl inflatable, sand, steel rivets | 147.5 x 147.5 x 239 cm | courtesy of the artist

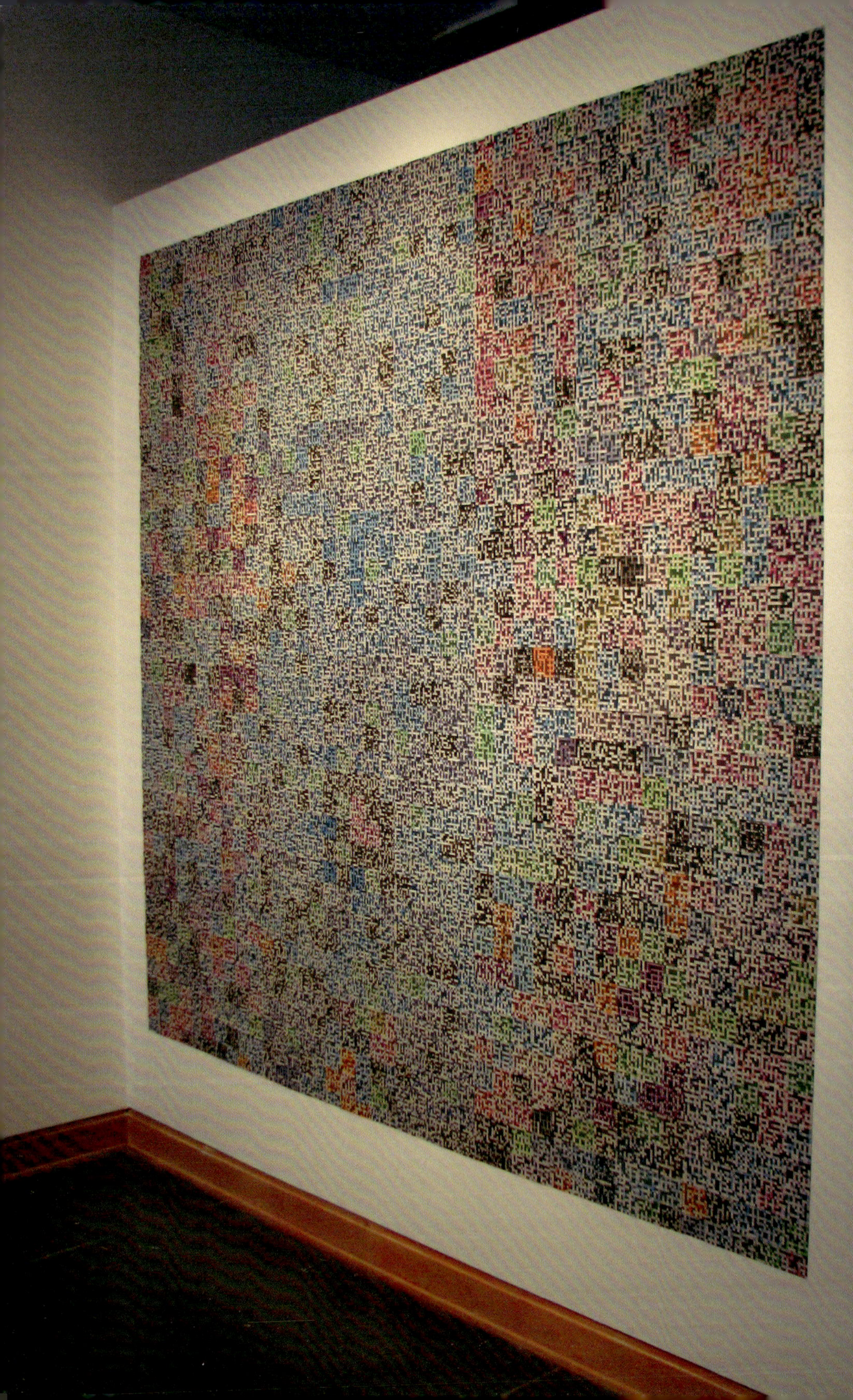

TYLER HODGINS, a Victoria-based artist, works primarily in sculpture, however his portfolio includes video, photography, and installation works, as well as public art. He graduated in 1990 from the Victoria College of Art diploma program and was named an honorary associate of the college in 1993. He was the recipient of the BC Arts Council Project Assistance grant for visual artists in 2001 and 2002. He has also competed as a finalist in numerous public art competitions, including 2010 "Mapping and Marking" Olympic and Paralympics Games (Vancouver), Cloverdale Public Art (Surrey), Harbourfront Plaza Public Art (Nanaimo), Bastion Square and Memorial Arena (Victoria), among others. Hodgins has not only exhibited his artworks in public spaces but has also been included in various solo and group shows. Some recent public projects include Glass Half Full (Holland Point Park, Victoria, BC, 2011), Watch This Space (Calgary, AB, 2010, and Victoria, BC, 2011), and Gateway (Richmond, BC, 2010). He has notably exhibited Who's Afraid of Red, Yellow, and Blue (Stride Gallery, Calgary, AB, 2010), The Storage Room and The Corridor (Deluge Contemporary Art, Victoria, BC, 2010), and Please Try Again (Kelowna Art Gallery, Kelowna, BC, 2009). His group shows include The Lost Art of LP Covers (Deluge Contemporary Art, Victoria, BC, 2007–2011), Fantasy Island (Slide Room Gallery, VISA, Victoria, BC, 2010), Public Realm (Propeller Centre for the Arts, Toronto, ON, 2010), Wish List (Polychrome Fine Arts, Victoria, BC, 2009), and Flow (Truck Gallery, Calgary, AB, 2006).

Hodgins' studio projects typically focus on themes of home, language, repetition/reproduction, and chance. His public works often act as a tool for seeing or framing an environment, with an emphasis on interactivity, collaboration, and the importance of "place."

Tyler Hodgins | installation view, *Please Try Again*, 2009 | losing crossword scratch tickets, donation box | 259 x 259 cm approx. | courtesy of the artist

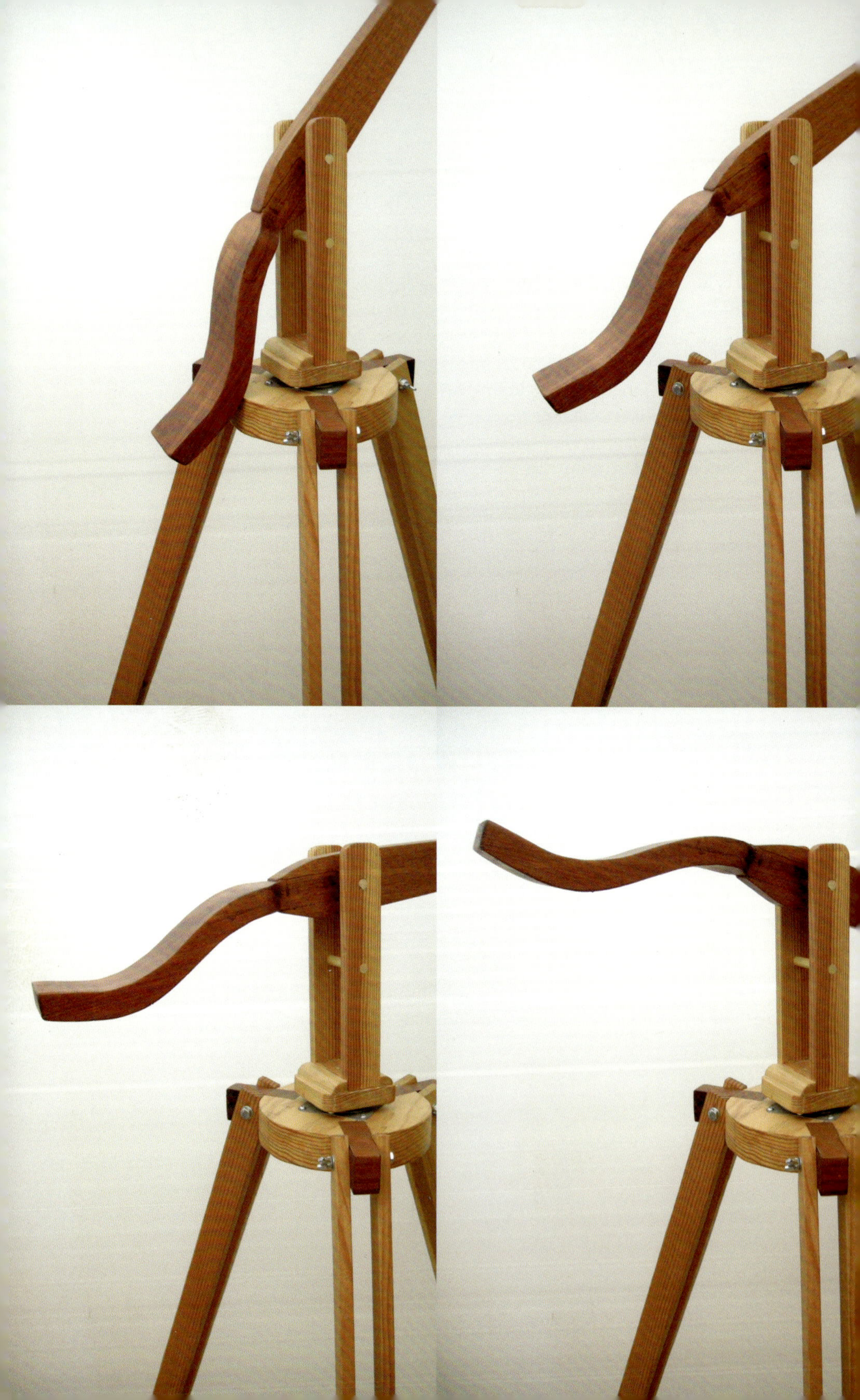

ALISON MACTAGGART is a Vancouver-based artist and educator. She completed an MFA at York University, a BFA at Simon Fraser University, and a diploma in Visual Arts at Camosun College in Victoria. She has received awards and grants from the BC Arts Council, Social Sciences and Humanities Research Council, and the Canada Council for the Arts. She currently teaches in the Fine Arts Department at Kwantlen Polytechnic University in Surrey, BC. Recent exhibitions include Game Show (Surrey Art Gallery, Surrey, BC, 2010) and a variation of Promising Objects (University of Lethbridge Art Gallery, Lethbridge, AB, 2010). In 2012, she is participating in an exhibition at Vancouver Access Artist Run Centre as part of the centre's 20th anniversary.

MacTaggart's conceptually inspired installation work bridges the disciplines of sculpture, drawing, and writing. Her work evolves from both personal and conceptual concerns; although not always explicitly expressed in the material embodiment of the work, these concerns directly inform their making. She is as interested in the ideas that inspire a project as she is in the process, materials, and craft that bring them to fruition.

Alison MacTaggart | details, *The Egg Throwing Apparatus*, 2002/2012 | wood, hardware watercolour on paper | dimensions variable | courtesy of the artist

WENDY WELCH is a Victoria-based artist, art writer, curator, and educator, as well as the founder and director of the Vancouver Island School of Art. She studied visual art at the University of Victoria (MFA), California State University in Los Angeles, and Concordia University, Montreal (BFA). Her work has been presented at the Southern Alberta Art Gallery, the Art Gallery of Greater Victoria, and the Richmond Art Gallery, among other galleries and artist-run centres. Recent solo and group exhibitions include Circuitous Routes: Abundance/Excess (Open Space, Victoria, BC, 2009) and Push/Pull (Produce Gallery, San Diego, CA, 2008). She has taught at the Camosun College, the Victoria College of Art and the University of Victoria. She was the visual arts writer for Monday Magazine (a Victoria-based weekly) from 2002 to 2008. Her writing has been published in Artichoke, Border Crossings and Canadian Art and in catalogue essays for Open Space, the New Gallery and the Nanaimo Art Gallery. In her art practice, Welch works with everyday materials and found objects that take form as installation, sculpture, painting, and drawing.

LIST OF WORKS

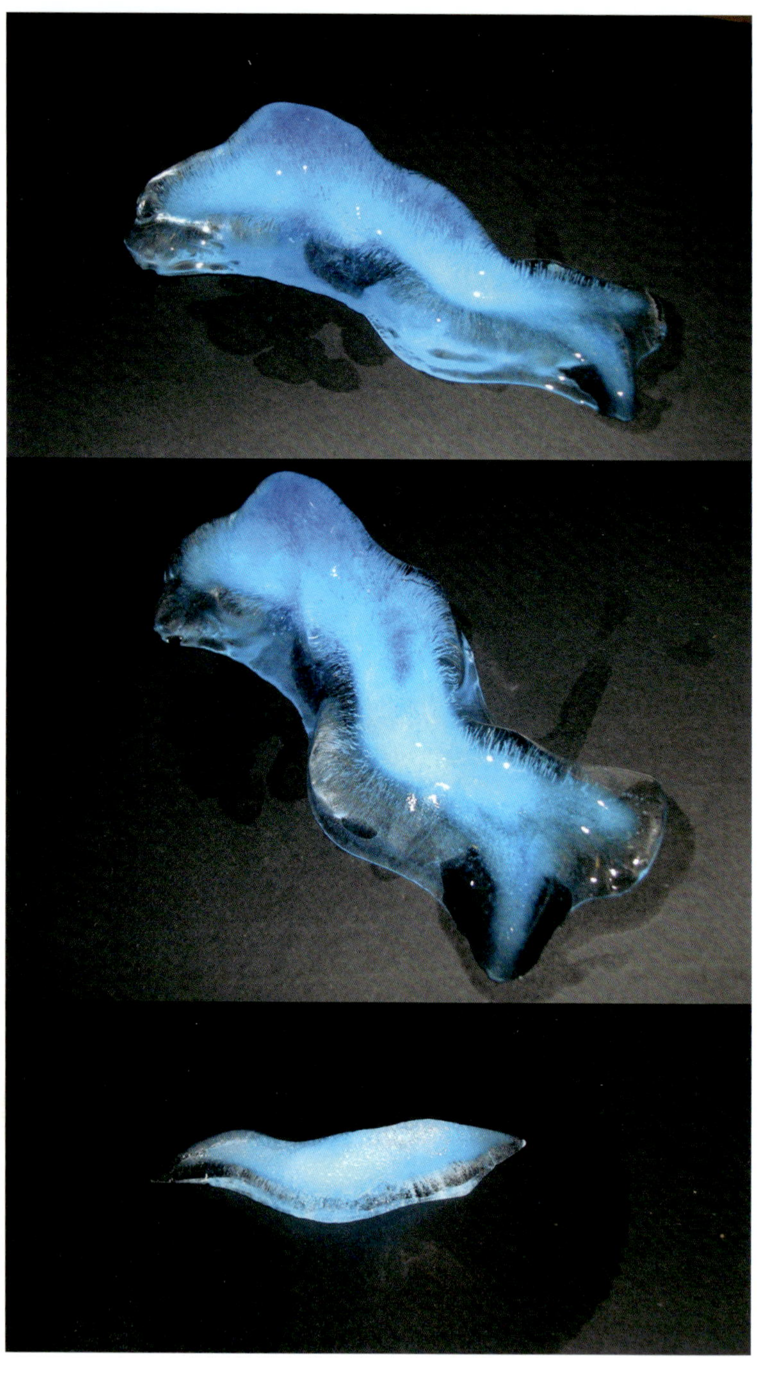

Tyler Hodgins | Study for *Sleeping Bag*, 2012 | cast ice, food colouring | dimensions variable | courtesy of the artist

SONNY ASSU

We Wai Kai (Warrior #1), 2011
archival pigment print
38 x 49 cm

Wise Ones (Elder #1), 2011
archival pigment print
38 x 49 cm

Wise Ones (Elder #2), 2011
archival pigment print
38 x 49 cm

Wise Ones (Elder #3), 2011
archival pigment print
38 x 49 cm

Wise Ones (Elder #4), 2011
archival pigment print
38 x 49 cm

Longing #2 , #3 and #8, 2011
found cedar and brass
dimensions variable

All works courtesy of the artist and Equinox Gallery

SONNY ASSU AND ERIC DEIS

Museum of Anthropology, 2011
archival pigment print
71 x 106.5 cm

Equinox Gallery, 2011
archival pigment print
71 x 106.5 cm

Roberts Gallery and Gifts, 2011
archival pigment print
71 x 106.5 cm

All works in this series courtesy of the artists

GREGORY BALL

You Suck! (2009/2012)
video installation, drawings mixed media on vellum
dimensions variable
courtesy of the artist

MEGAN DICKIE

Step into the Ring, 2012
4-channel video
dimensions variable

Submission, 2012
leather, vinyl inflatable, foam, leadshot
106.5 x 76 x 213.5 cm

The Tangler, 2010
leather, vinyl inflatable, sand, steel rivets
147.5 x 147.5 x 239 cm
Produced with generous support from the B.C. Arts Council

Tussle with the Tangler, 2012
4-channel video, dimensions variable

All works courtesy of the artist

TYLER HODGINS

Please Try Again, 2009
losing crossword scratch tickets, donation box
259 x 259 cm approx.
courtesy of the artist

Sleeping Bag, 2012
sculptural intervention, cast ice, food colouring
dimensions variable

ALISON MACTAGGART

The Egg Throwing Apparatus, 2002/2012
wood, hardware, watercolour on paper
dimensions variable
courtesy of the artist

CREDITS

Curator: Nicole Stanbridge
Contributors: Nicole Stanbridge, Wendy Welch
Publication Project Manager: Nicole Stanbridge
Editor: Audrey McClellan
Publication Design: Ross Macaulay
Printed in Canada by Friesens Corp.

Thank you to the AGGV staff for their contributions to the success of this exhibition, to Ross Macaulay and Audrey McClellan for their creativity and contributions to this publication, and to all the artists, arts administrators, art educators, and cultural workers who tirelessly throw down for their communities.

Canada Council   Conseil des Arts
for the Arts   du Canada

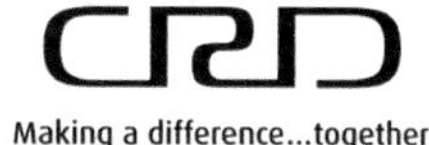

Making a difference...together

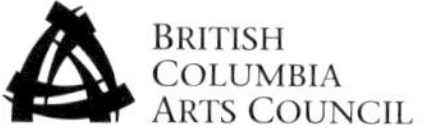

BRITISH
COLUMBIA
ARTS COUNCIL

A R T GALLERY

O F   G R E A T E R   V I C T O R I A

Art Gallery of Greater Victoria
1040 Moss Street
Victoria, British Columbia
Canada V8V 4P1
1.250.384.4171 aggv.ca